W9-AQK-965

3 9082 04871377 E

64184

3

15.27

INKSTER PUBLIC LIBRARY
2005 INKSTER ROAD
INKSTER, MICHIGAN 48141

Cornerstones of Freedom

The Hindenburg Disaster

R. Conrad Stein

CHILDRENS PRESS®
CHICAGO

INKSTER PUBLIC LIBRARY
2005 INKSTER ROAD
INKSTER, MICHIGAN 48141

3 9082 04891377 9

Library of Congress Cataloging-in-Publication Data

Stein, R. Conrad.
 Hindenburg disaster / by R. Conrad Stein.
  p. cm. — (Cornerstones of freedom)
 Summary: Describes the development and early flights
of airships and the disastrous crash of the Hindenburg
at an airfield in New Jersey in 1937.
 ISBN 0-516-06663-3
 1. Hindenburg (Airship)—Juvenile literature.
2. Aeronautics—Accidents—1937—Juvenile literature.
[1. Hindenburg (Airship) 2. Airships. 3. Aeronautics—
Accidents.] I. Title. II. Series.
TL659.H5S74 1993
363.12'465—dc20   92-34520
                                                        CIP
                                                         AC

Copyright 1993 by Childrens Press®, Inc.
All rights reserved. Published simultaneously in Canada.
Printed in the United States of America.
1 2 3 4 5 6 7 8 9 10 R 02 01 00 99 98 97 96 95 94 93

Thursday, May 6, 1937.

Excited passengers on the German dirigible *Hindenburg* gazed down on New York City. "Look," said a man on the *Hindenburg*'s observation deck. "There's the Empire State Building." The graceful airship flew so close to the recently completed tower that the *Hindenburg*'s passengers could see people waving to them from the building's top floors.

New Yorkers staring at the great craft as it glided through the sky saw black swastikas clearly painted on its tailfins. Adolf Hitler and the Nazi party had risen to power in Germany in

The Hindenburg *passing over New York City on May 6, 1937*

Adolf Hitler

1933. The German leader insisted on putting the Nazi symbol on all aircraft and ships made in his country. The *Hindenburg* was the pride of modern Germany, so the swastika was strikingly displayed. Ironically, the airship was named after Paul von Hindenburg, Germany's last elected president before Hitler became dictator.

The *Hindenburg* was an amazing ship. Cigar shaped, it stretched as long as three football fields. On this voyage, it carried ninety-seven people—thirty-six passengers and sixty-one crew members. Flying at an average speed of eighty-five miles per hour, it was able to complete a trip from Europe to the United States in less than four days. At the time, steamships took up to four weeks to cross the Atlantic Ocean. On May 3, 1937, the monster airship had taken off from Frankfurt, Germany. Its destination was a landing field in Lakehurst, New Jersey. So far, the trip had been routine.

South of New York City, the scenery grew less spectacular. Passengers crowded into the smoking room to have a last cigarette before landing. It was only in the smoking room that people on board became mindful that they were completely surrounded by highly combustible hydrogen gas. The tiniest flame could ignite the hydrogen and cause a devastating explosion. But the German engineers who built the *Hindenburg* and other passenger-carrying dirigibles had taken

A lounge area aboard the Hindenburg

extraordinary precautions against sparks or accidental flames. Hallways and ladders were rubber coated to reduce static electricity. All matches and cigarettes were taken from passengers when they came on board. Cigarette lighters in the smoking room were chained to furniture so no careless person could light up in the wrong place.

Because of these measures, German-made dirigibles enjoyed a remarkable safety record. The *Hindenburg* and her sister ships had completed hundreds of Atlantic crossings and carried thousands of passengers without a mishap. German engineering had been prominent in airship development since the time

Ferdinand von Zeppelin

of Count Ferdinand von Zeppelin, who was sometimes affectionately called "that Crazy Old Count." The count earned his nickname because of his single-minded devotion to airships.

Zeppelin was born in 1838 into a family of wealthy German landholders. As a twenty-three-year-old army officer, he journeyed to the United States to observe American soldiers fighting the Civil War. At an army post in St. Paul, Minnesota, Union officers invited him to ride a hot-air balloon. Zeppelin found the flight exhilarating, but while soaring through the air, he kept

Count von Zeppelin became fascinated with lighter-than-air vehicles after riding in a hot-air balloon during the American Civil War.

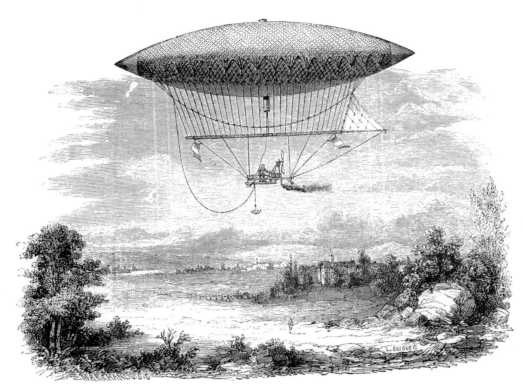

A lighter-than-air craft built in the 1850s by French engineer Henri Giffard

pondering the question, "Why can't we steer this balloon? If we could steer the balloon rather than just letting it drift in the winds, we could work miracles."

For the rest of his life, Zeppelin worked to build a powered balloon that could be steered in flight. He and others began using the word *dirigible* to describe the powered-balloon concept. *Dirigible* comes from a Latin word that means "to steer" or "to direct."

Although he became a master at airship design, Zeppelin was not the first man to put a dirigible into the skies. As early as 1852, a French engineer named Henri Giffard built a lighter-than-air craft that he flew seventeen miles from

Henri Giffard

7

The metal framework of an early zeppelin

Paris to the city of Trappes. Some thirty years later, French inventors Charles Renard and Arthur Krebs constructed an airship powered by an electric motor. Another dirigible pioneer was Brazilian-born Alberto Santos-Dumont.

In 1900, at the age of sixty-two, Zeppelin flew his first dirigible. It was a huge craft, shaped like a sausage and measuring 425 feet in length. Onlookers gasped when they saw it on the ground. Surely, they thought, this giant would not be able to take to the air. To everyone's astonishment, Zeppelin's machine rose and flew. Its first flight lasted only ten minutes, however, before it buckled in the middle and bounced to the earth.

Undaunted, Zeppelin built another airship, then another and another. Each craft was an improvement over the previous one. Zeppelin was the first to construct an airship with a metal framework. The framework allowed the airship to maintain its shape even when it wasn't filled with gas. For this reason, this new type of airship was called a rigid airship. In 1910, Zeppelin began taking people aloft, offering them thrilling sightseeing rides. Soon his dirigibles were competing with trains and ships by carrying passengers from city to city. By 1914, the year he died, Zeppelin controlled a fleet of thirty airships. Dirigibles were so closely identified with the

Passengers boarding a German zeppelin in 1919

Crazy Old Count that all over the world, rigid airships were called *zeppelins*.

The same year that Zeppelin died, a young student shot and killed Archduke Ferdinand, heir to the throne of Austria-Hungary. The assassination triggered World War I, the most destructive war in history. The German military soon found a new use for Zeppelin's wondrous airships.

Panic gripped London in early 1915 as citizens scrambled about the streets, screaming in horror. Above them, German zeppelins hovered in the sky, raining bombs on the helpless city. The Londoners were suffering through one of history's first air raids. Early in the war, the British had no defenses against these terror attacks from the sky. In all, the zeppelins made 51 raids over British cities, dropping nearly 200 tons of bombs and killing 557 people. The British

A diagram of the type of zeppelin used by the Germans in air raids against the British during World War I

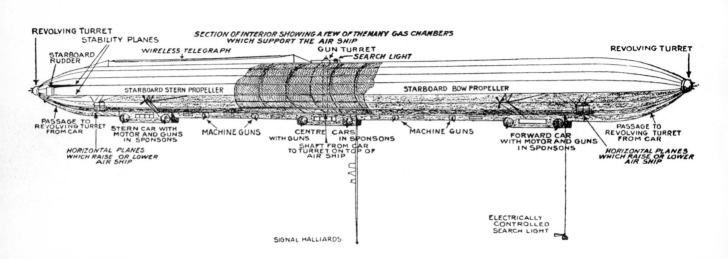

REVOLVING TURRET
STABILITY PLANES
SECTION OF INTERIOR SHOWING A FEW OF THE MANY GAS CHAMBERS WHICH SUPPORT THE AIR SHIP
REVOLVING TURRET
STARBOARD RUDDER
WIRELESS TELEGRAPH
GUN TURRET
SEARCH LIGHT

STARBOARD STERN PROPELLER
STARBOARD BOW PROPELLER

PASSAGE TO REVOLVING TURRET FROM CAR
STERN CAR WITH MOTOR AND GUNS IN SPONSONS
MACHINE GUNS
CENTRE CARS WITH GUNS
CARS IN SPONSONS
MACHINE GUNS
FORWARD CAR WITH MOTOR AND GUNS IN SPONSONS
PASSAGE TO REVOLVING TURRET FROM CAR

HORIZONTAL PLANES WHICH RAISE OR LOWER AIR SHIP
SHAFT FROM CAR TO TURRET ON TOP OF AIR SHIP
HORIZONTAL PLANES WHICH RAISE OR LOWER AIR SHIP

ELECTRICALLY CONTROLLED SEARCH LIGHT

SIGNAL HALLIARDS

*Opposite page:
Construction of
the* Graf Zeppelin
Left: The Graf
Zeppelin *flying
over London's
Wembley Stadium
in 1930*

a German company launched the *Graf Zeppelin,*
a magnificent airship named after the Crazy Old
Count (*Graf* is the German word for "count").
Before it was retired, the *Graf Zeppelin* made 144
Atlantic crossings, logged more than 1 million
miles, and carried some 18,000 passengers in
comfort and safety.

The *Graf Zeppelin*'s success was achieved despite the fact that it used highly flammable hydrogen as a lighter-than-air lifting material. Helium was another lighter-than-air gas that could be used to lift dirigibles. Helium was much safer than hydrogen because it was nonflammable. But helium was found only in five natural gas fields, all of which were located in the United States. In the 1930s, the American government had exclusive control over the

Spectators watched with interest as the Hindenburg *was pulled out of its hangar before its first test flight on May 13, 1936.*

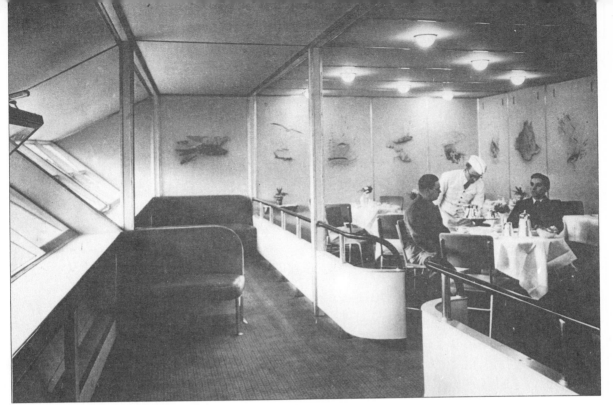

The dining room and promenade of the Hindenburg

helium trade. Remembering the terrifying raids
that zeppelins had made over Britain, American
authorities refused to send helium to Germany.

The helium-versus-hydrogen question did not
prevent the Germans from building the
Hindenburg, the grandest of all airships.
Completed in March 1936, it featured lavish
staterooms, a dance floor with a stage for a band,
a sprawling observation deck, and an elegant
dining room. At the time, the *Hindenburg* was
unrivaled as the queen of the skies.

Just after 7:00 P.M. on May 6, 1937, the
Hindenburg edged over its landing field at
Lakehurst, New Jersey. One of the people waiting

A Hindenburg
sleeping cabin

for the airship to arrive was Herbert Morrison, a radio reporter for station WLS in Chicago. *Hindenburg* landings were big news events because the airship often carried international celebrities. American actor Douglas Fairbanks and German world-heavyweight-boxing champion Max Schmeling had been recent passengers. On this trip, however, the *Hindenburg* carried no famous people, and Morrison thought his mission would be routine. In the night sky, he saw the sleek silver craft with the black swastikas on its stern. The four diesel engines that drove the airship's two propellers hummed steadily. Morrison began his broadcast:

"Well, here it comes, ladies and gentlemen, and what a sight it is, a thrilling one, a marvelous sight. . . . It's practically standing still now. They've dropped ropes out of the nose of the ship, and they've been taken ahold of on the field by a number of men. The vast motors of the ship are just holding it, just enough to keep it from . . ."

Then he paused, a pause that lasted two seconds.

"Oh, oh, oh! . . . It's burst into flames!" Morrison shouted. Terror ruled his voice. "Get out of the way, please, oh, my, this is terrible, oh my, get out of the way, please! It is burning, bursting into flames and is falling. . . . Oh! This is one of the worst. . . . Oh! Its a terrific sight. . . . Oh! . . It's crashing . . . bursting into flames, and

The Hindenburg *moments after catching fire*

it's falling on the mooring mast and all the folks between us. This is terrible," Morrison began to sob. "This is one of the worst catastrophes in the world."

W. W. Groves, a member of the ground crew, stood directly under the *Hindenburg*, looking up. He saw a small spark, "like static electricity," that danced along the ship's underbelly. "Look!" Groves said to the man next to him. The word

The exploding airship began crashing to the ground tail first.

had scarcely left his mouth when the *Hindenburg* exploded into a dazzling fireball. "The whole tail section burst into flame and I ran," Groves said later. "It was exploding above my head and fabric began to fall."

A motion-picture cameraman was filming the ground crew. Suddenly, he felt a terrific blast of heat. "Point the camera up!" his assistant shouted. The man trained his camera on the *Hindenburg*, which was now bathed in flames and crashing stern first. People, looking like tiny ants, were leaping from the airship onto the field. The cameraman filmed the entire scene as if hypnotized. Over and over he said, "Oh, my God! Oh, my God! Oh, my God!"

The *Hindenburg*'s captain, Max Pruss, heard a dim explosion and felt his ship sink to the stern. Instinctively, he grabbed the controls to level the craft. Then he heard the whoosh of fire. He released the controls, realizing at once that his ship was being consumed by flames, and that simply letting her crash would give the passengers a better chance of escape. His quick thinking saved dozens of lives.

Captain Max Pruss aboard the Hindenburg

People fled from the burning airship as it collapsed to the ground.

Joseph Spah, a passenger who was a circus acrobat by profession, was sitting in the dining room. In an instant, he was ringed by a circle of fire. Spah rushed to a window, but discovered that he could not open it. His movie camera had been dangling from his neck on a string. Using the camera as a club, he smashed at the windowpane until the glass shattered. Two men pushed ahead of him and climbed out of the broken window. Spah climbed out after them, and the three men clung to the outside of the ship. They had been in the bow of the ship, which was now pointed almost vertically in the air. Passengers in the stern had to jump only a few feet to safety, but those in the bow stared down at a deadly drop. After a few moments, the two men next to Spah could no longer hold on. They fell, screaming, to their deaths.

Spah knew that if he were to survive, he had to hold on until his section of the ship came closer to the ground. As he dangled, he remembered the many times he had risked his life in circus stunts. But this was no circus act. Screams from burned and dying people filled his ears. The window ledge grew unbearably hot, searing his hands. When he judged that he was about 40 feet from the ground, he let go, landed on the field, scrambled to his feet, and darted away to avoid being hit by falling debris. Amazingly, he suffered only a fractured heel in his fall.

Joseph Spah and his family just after the disaster

Mrs. Matilda Doehner, her husband, and her three children were on the observation deck when the walls around them erupted into fire. Mrs. Doehner screamed for her husband, but he had disappeared behind a sheet of flames. Instantly, the woman realized that the only way to save her children was to push them through the window. She swept six-year-old Werner into her arms and pressed him against the window. The pane fell out and Werner dropped to the ground. Then she pushed eight-year-old Walter through the opening. The boy's hair was on fire, but he was dragged to safety by a passenger who had already escaped. Mrs. Doehner shouted again for her husband and her fourteen-year-old daughter Irene, but no one answered her cry. With the furnacelike heat almost consuming her, she jumped out.

Once on the ground, the airship was entirely consumed by flames.

Werner Franz

The most miraculous escape was that of Werner Franz, a fourteen-year-old cabin boy. Franz was walking in the belly of the *Hindenburg* when the hydrogen gas exploded. Completely enveloped by fire, Franz said his prayers, certain he would die. Then, above him, a tank burst, soaking him with water. At that same moment, his section of the ship crashed to the ground. The water gave Franz a temporary shield from the fire, and he picked his way through the wreckage. He emerged, his hair and eyebrows singed, but otherwise unhurt.

Other people were not so lucky.

Some men and women walked like zombies out of the flaming inferno. They were naked, their bodies black with burns. One man ran from the wreck completely on fire. Members of the ground crew could not believe that the man was still alive, as he seemed to be a ball of orange flames. Finally, the man fell. The flames devouring him were so intense that ten minutes elapsed before rescuers could approach his charred body.

Fred Tobin

During the fiery crash, acts of heroism were so common that they went almost unnoticed. United States Navy chief Fred "Bull" Tobin commanded the ground crew. When he saw the *Hindenburg* mushroom into flame above him, he shouted in a booming foghorn voice, "Stand fast, men. We have to help those people inside."

Members of the rescue squad attempt to help a badly burned victim.

Smoke billows from the site of the fiery wreckage.

Risking their lives, the ground crew remained under the burning airship. Many of the passengers who jumped from the dying craft fell literally into the arms of the waiting crew. Captain Pruss helped seven men in the control car escape through a window. Pruss dragged an unconscious crew member to safety, even though his own hair and clothes were on fire.

Exactly thirty-four seconds after the first burst of fire, the *Hindenburg* lay on the ground. Its metal framework—all that was left of the ship— was twisted into a hideous, flaming skeleton. A photographer later called the crash "a moment of spectacular madness." For the people who survived the holocaust, the thirty-four-second span seemed like an eternity.

On the field, stunned reporter Herbert Morrison continued his broadcast: "This is terrible . . . Oh, the humanity and all the passengers . . . a mass of flaming wreckage. Honestly, I can hardly breathe. . . . I'm going to step inside where I can't see it. . . . It's terrible . . . I . . . Folks, I'm going to have to stop for a moment because I've lost my voice. This is the worst thing I've ever witnessed."

When it was all over, a hideous, twisted shell was all that was left of the once-magnificent airship.

The survivors gathered in dazed groups. Wives looked for husbands. Relatives who had driven to Lakehurst to pick up family members now desperately shouted their names. Mrs. Doehner, who had thrown her children out of the observation deck window, hugged her two young sons. They had survived the crash. Mrs. Doehner's hair was burned to its roots, but she hardly felt the pain. She learned that her husband was dead and that her daughter, Irene, was badly burned. Irene died a short time later.

Some surviving crew members pose in front of the wreckage.

Left: The front page of a Chicago newspaper on the evening of the crash
Above: Ernst Lehmann

In all, thirty-six people—twenty-two crew members, thirteen passengers, and one man on the ground—died in the *Hindenburg* disaster. One of the casualties was Captain Ernst Lehmann, the *Hindenburg*'s commander. He had been aboard the airship even though it was being captained by Pruss on this trip. Lehmann walked away from the wreckage, but died of burns several hours later. Among his last words were, *"Ich kann es nicht verstehen"*—"I can't understand it."

Germans stop to look at a newspaper extra announcing the tragedy.

Around the world, experts on airship
operations also failed to understand the terrible
crash. How did this magnificent airship—in the
hands of a skilled crew—end up a fiery wreck?
Many people concluded that the ship had been
struck by lightning. A rain had fallen over
Lakehurst earlier that day, and the possibility of
lightning had been present. Other experts
suggested that static electricity was the culprit.
Although the craft had endless safeguards against
static discharges, there was no foolproof way to
eliminate all errant sparks. Finally, some people
believed that the *Hindenburg* had been a victim
of sabotage.

Charges that the airship had been destroyed by foul play echoed long after its last, fatal flight. Writing in the early 1970s, one author theorized that an anti-Nazi crew member had placed a time bomb inside the craft. This crewman, the author maintained, wanted to discredit Adolf Hitler and the Nazis by devastating Germany's showcase vehicle. Other investigators, however, disagreed that sabotage had brought the ship down.

The *Hindenburg* tragedy became etched in the memory of the 1930s public largely because it was the first disaster of great magnitude that was captured on film. In those days, when there was no television, people watched news segments at their neighborhood movie theaters. Newsreel cameras captured nearly every flaming second of

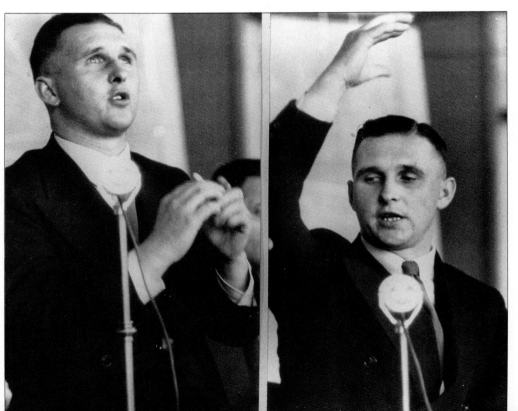

Helmut Lau, a crew member who was in the stern of the airship and saw the fire break out, tells his story to a committee investigating the cause of the disaster.

Radio announcer Herbert Morrison (on right) listens to a recording of his famous newscast of the terrible event.

the ship's destruction. The film, coupled with the recorded voice of radio announcer Herbert Morrison, was released to movie theaters just days after the event. Moviegoers gasped, and many screamed, when they saw the mighty airship go down in a fearful blaze while badly burned passengers struggled to escape.

The terrible crash at Lakehurst ended the era of passenger-carrying airships. Few people, after witnessing the disaster on film, wanted to travel on zeppelins. After the disaster, airships were used as patrol craft by the United States Navy, and even today, huge blimps are used by private companies to display advertising messages. But no longer would sleek zeppelins outfitted with luxurious passenger quarters float vacationers effortlessly over the oceans.

Those who were alive during the 1930s will never forget the crash of the world's greatest airship. It was one of the decade's most spectacular and horrifying news stories. Even today, watching the newsreel film of the tragedy and hearing Morrison's emotionally charged voice is a chilling experience: "This is terrible . . . Oh, the humanity and all the passengers . . . This is the worst thing I've ever witnessed."

Captain Pruss lays a wreath at a Hindenburg *memorial in Frankfurt, Germany, on the tenth anniversary of the tragedy.*

INDEX

PHOTO CREDITS

Cover, 1, The Bettmann Archive; 2, AP/Wide World; 3, UPI/Bettmann; 4, AP/Wide World; 5, University of Texas, History of Aviation Collection; 6 (both photos), 7 (bottom), The Bettmann Archive; 7 (top), Historical Pictures/Stock Montage; 8, North Wind; 9, UPI/Bettmann; 10, North Wind; 11, Imperial War Museum, London; 12, AP/Wide World; 13, 14, 15 (top), UPI/Bettmann; 15 (bottom), University of Texas, History of Aviation Collection; 17, AP/Wide World; 18, 19 (top), University of Texas, History of Aviation Collection; 19 (bottom), AP/Wide World; 21, 22 (top), UPI/Bettmann; 22 (bottom), 23 (top), AP/Wide World; 23 (bottom), UPI/Bettmann; 24, AP/Wide World; 25, UPI/Bettmann; 26, 27 (right), University of Texas, History of Aviation Collection; 27 (left), Historical Pictures/Stock Montage; 28, AP/Wide World; 29, UPI/Bettmann; 30, 31, AP/Wide World

Picture Identifications:
Cover: The explosion of the *Hindenburg* on May 6, 1937
Page 1: The *Hindenburg* landing in Germany after a two-day flight
Page 2: The *Hindenburg* passing by New York's Empire State Building on its way to landing in New Jersey after a trip from Germany

Project Editor: Shari Joffe
Designer: Karen Yops
Photo Editor: Jan Izzo
Cornerstones of Freedom Logo: David Cunningham

ABOUT THE AUTHOR

R. Conrad Stein was born and raised in Chicago. He enlisted in the U.S. Marine Corps at age eighteen and served for three years. He then attended the University of Illinois, where he received a B.A. in history. He later studied in Mexico, earning an advanced degree from the University of Guanajuato.

Mr. Stein is the author of many books, articles, and short stories for young people. He lives in Chicago with his wife and their daughter Janna.